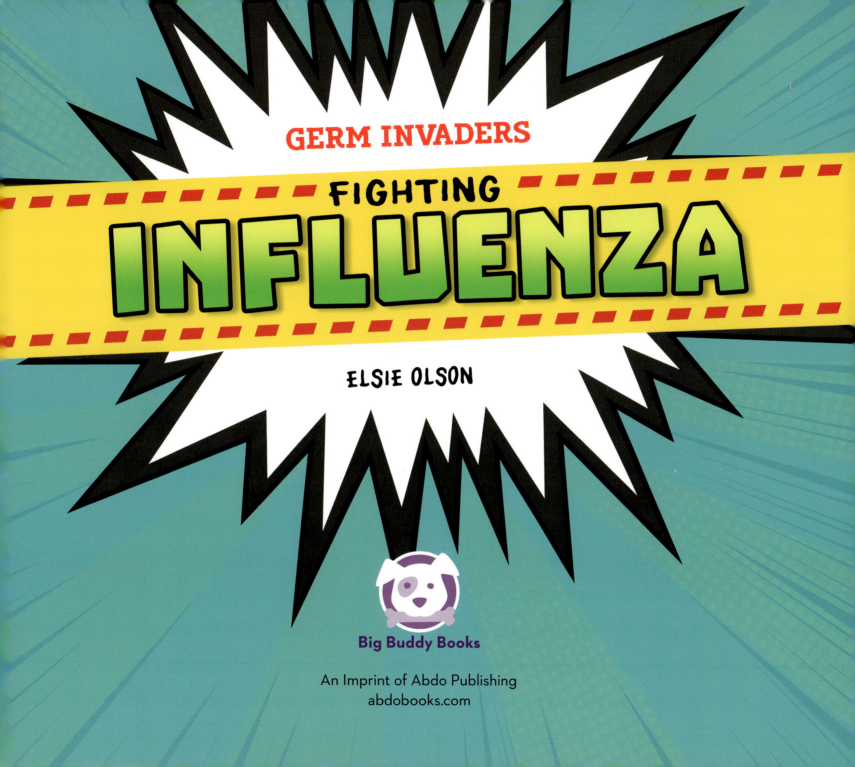

GERM INVADERS

FIGHTING INFLUENZA

ELSIE OLSON

Big Buddy Books

An Imprint of Abdo Publishing
abdobooks.com

abdobooks.com

Published by Abdo Publishing, a division of ABDO, PO Box 398166, Minneapolis, Minnesota 55439. Copyright © 2021 by Abdo Consulting Group, Inc. International copyrights reserved in all countries. No part of this book may be reproduced in any form without written permission from the publisher. Big Buddy Books™ is a trademark and logo of Abdo Publishing.

Printed in the United States of America, North Mankato, Minnesota
102020
012021

Design: Sarah DeYoung, Mighty Media, Inc.
Production: Mighty Media, Inc.
Editor: Rebecca Felix

Cover Photographs: Shutterstock (all)
Interior Photographs: SAS Scandinavian Airlines/Wikimedia, p. 26; Shutterstock, pp. 5–9, 12–13, 15, 17, 19–20, 23–27, 29
Design Elements: Shutterstock (all)

Library of Congress Control Number: 2020940293

Publisher's Cataloging-in-Publication Data
Names: Olson, Elsie, author.
Title: Fighting influenza / by Elsie Olson
Description: Minneapolis, Minnesota : Abdo Publishing, 2021 | Series: Germ invaders | Includes online resources and index
Identifiers: ISBN 9781532194238 (lib. bdg.) | ISBN 9781098213596 (ebook)
Subjects: LCSH: Influenza viruses--Juvenile literature. | Influenza--Prevention--Juvenile literature. | Health behavior--Juvenile literature. | Immunology--Juvenile literature. | Hygiene--Juvenile literature. | Viruses--Juvenile literature.
Classification: DDC 616.079--dc23

CONTENTS

Your Amazing Body..4

When the Flu Attacks...6

All about the Flu...8

Pandemic! 10

Catching the Flu...12

Flu Season 14

Do You Have the Flu?...16

Getting Better 20

When to See a Doctor..22

Flu Complications 24

The Flu Vaccine 26

Healthy Habits...28

Glossary 30

Online Resources 31

Index..32

YOUR AMAZING BODY

You are amazing! So is your body. Most of the time your body works just fine. But sometimes germs **invade** it. Germs can make you sick. Every year, germs cause millions of people get sick with influenza, or the flu.

GET TO KNOW GERMS

Germs are tiny **organisms**. They can live inside people, plants, and animals. There are four main types of germs.

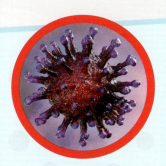

VIRUSES

Viruses are parasitic. This means they cannot survive on their own. They require a host cell to reproduce. Influenza is caused by viruses.

BACTERIA

Bacteria are single-celled creatures. They can survive on their own or inside another living organism.

PROTOZOA

Protozoa are single-celled creatures. Some can survive on their own. Others are parasitic.

FUNGI

Fungi are plant-like organisms. They get their food from people, plants, and animals.

WHEN THE FLU ATTACKS

Flu viruses are very simple **organisms**. They are no more than **particles** containing **RNA**. But these small organisms can cause big trouble when they **invade** your body.

INVASION

A sick person coughs, sneezes, or talks near you. Their germs enter the air. You breathe in the virus.

FINDING A HOST

The flu virus attaches to a host cell inside your nose or **sinuses**.

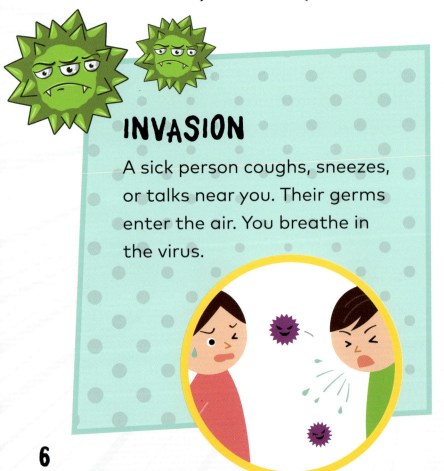

REPLICATION

The flu virus **releases** its **genetic** material into the host cell. The virus orders the cell to make copies of the virus.

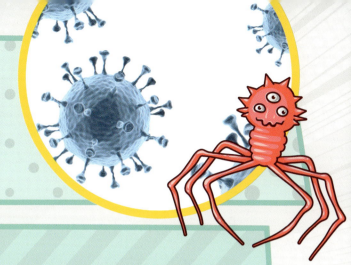

SPREADING

The virus copies spread throughout the body. They find host cells and continue to make copies. Any time you cough or sneeze, you release virus **particles** into the air. Now the virus can **infect** other people.

FIGHTING BACK

Your immune system fights the virus.
- White blood cells attack the virus.
- Your body temperature may increase, causing a fever. This helps kill the virus.

Thanks to their immune systems, most people recover from the flu within two weeks.

ALL ABOUT THE FLU

There are many types of flu viruses. All types attack your respiratory system. This system functions to allow breathing. It includes the nose, throat, and lungs.

Each year, between 9 million and 49 million Americans get the flu. Most recover. But the flu can be harmful in very young children and elderly adults.

FLU OR STOMACH FLU?

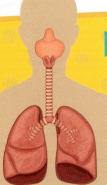

Influenza is not the stomach flu. Different viruses cause each illness. Influenza attacks your respiratory system. The stomach flu attacks your stomach and intestines.

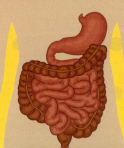

Some types of flu cause more harm than others.

PANDEMIC!

Flu **symptoms** are mentioned in a **text** that is more than 2,000 years old! But the first confirmed **evidence** of the flu is from Europe and Africa in 1580.

Some flu virus types are especially **contagious** and deadly. These types can cause a **pandemic**. From 1918 to 1919, a serious flu pandemic swept the globe.

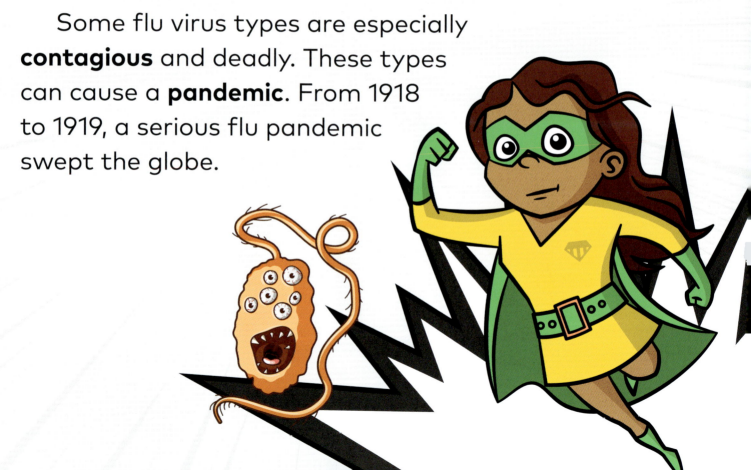

MODERN PANDEMICS

1918 SPANISH FLU
- Originated in birds, then passed to people
- Killed at least 50 million people

1981 HIV/AIDS
- Human Immunodeficiency Virus/Acquired Immune Deficiency Syndrome
- Since discovery in 1981, has killed 32 million people

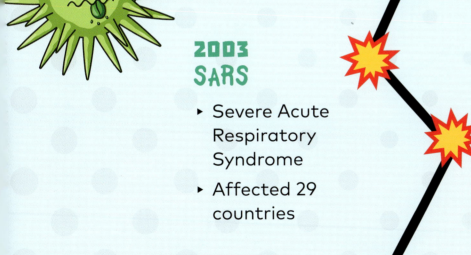

2003 SARS
- Severe Acute Respiratory Syndrome
- Affected 29 countries

2019 COVID-19
- Caused by a virus called SARS-CoV-2
- Spread to more than 200 countries

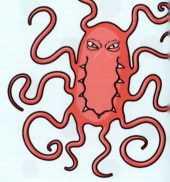

11

CATCHING THE FLU

The flu spreads through tiny droplets. When someone with the flu talks, coughs, or sneezes, they **release** these droplets into the air. Then, other people breathe in the droplets.

The flu virus can also survive for several hours on surfaces such as doorknobs and countertops. If you touch **infected** surfaces and then touch your nose, mouth, or eyes, the virus can enter your body.

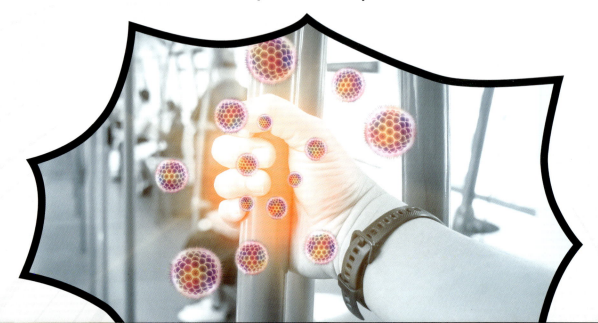

The flu often spreads in crowded places. These include buses, trains, schools, and workplaces.

FLU SEASON

Flu season is the time of year when the flu is most common. On Earth's northern **hemisphere**, this is from October to May. The air is colder and drier there during these months. Flu viruses survive better in these conditions. Earth's southern hemisphere sees colder, drier weather in opposite months. Flu season there is from April to September.

In the United States, flu season peaks in winter months.

DO YOU HAVE THE FLU?

Flu **symptoms** begin about two days after **infection**. But you can be **contagious** before symptoms begin!

Flu symptoms include tiredness, fever, and headache. Many people also experience a cough or sore throat. Some have chills or muscle aches.

It is important to stay home from school and other activities when you have the flu. You are contagious for five to seven days after showing symptoms.

Some people think they have the flu when they really have a cold. These illnesses share common **symptoms**. However, flu symptoms are usually worse than cold symptoms.

The only way to know for sure if you have the flu is to have your doctor give you a special test. But most people never take this test. Instead, they just treat the symptoms. The flu and colds share some similar treatments.

FLU OR COLD?

These illnesses share many symptoms. But some symptoms are more common of the flu.

BOTH

Sore Throat   Runny Nose

Tiredness   Cough

Sneezing

FLU

Fever   Chills and Sweats

Extreme Exhaustion

Colds are more common than the flu. Some people catch more than eight colds in a year!

GETTING BETTER

Most cases of the flu can be treated at home. Rest lets your immune system do its work. Staying home will also keep you from spreading the flu to others.

Sleep helps your body fight the flu. So does drinking lots of fluids. Clear fluids, such as water, apple juice, and broth are best.

If you must leave your home while you have the flu, wear a face mask to protect others.

MEDICATIONS AND REMEDIES

Some **over-the-counter** medicine and at-home remedies can help control your flu **symptoms**.

SYMPTOM	MEDICINE	REMEDY
Sore throat	Pain reliever / Throat spray or lozenges	Hot water with honey / Cold foods
Headache or muscle aches	Pain reliever	Warm compress / Warm bath with Epsom salts
Dry cough	Cough suppressant / Cough drops	Hot water with honey / Breathing steam
Cough with **mucus**	Cough expectorant	Hot water, tea, or soup / Breathing steam
Stuffy nose	Nasal decongestant / Nasal spray	Peppermint tea / Warm compress / Breathing steam

WHEN TO SEE A DOCTOR

Your flu will likely go away within one or two weeks. But sometimes the flu leads to **complications**. Some people are at a higher risk for these. This includes people under age 5 or over age 64, pregnant women, and people with **chronic** medical conditions.

If you are in a high-risk group and think you have the flu, call your doctor. Flu complications can cause more serious illnesses.

Today, many doctor's appointments can be done over video chat.

FLU COMPLICATIONS

BRONCHITIS

Bronchial tubes move air in the lungs. The flu can **inflame** these tubes. This is called bronchitis. Its signs include coughing up **mucus**, chest tightness, and shortness of breath.

EAR INFECTION

The flu can cause liquid to get trapped in the ear. This can cause an **infection**. Its signs include ear pain, trouble hearing, and liquid draining from the ear.

SINUS INFECTION

The flu can cause **sinuses** to swell and trap liquid. This can cause a sinus **infection**. Its signs include pressure around the eyes and cheeks and yellow or green **mucus** from the nose.

PNEUMONIA

Pneumonia is an infection of the lungs. Its signs include coughing, chest pain, and trouble breathing.

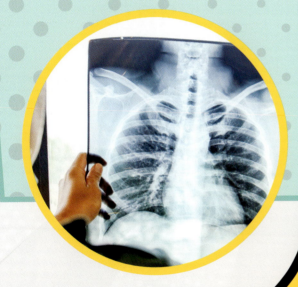

If you have **symptoms** of any of these illnesses, call your doctor right away!

THE FLU VACCINE

The flu vaccine can help protect you against the flu. This shot gives you a small dose of flu viruses. It **exposes** your immune system to these viruses. This prepares your body to fight the viruses if you come in contact with them again.

Most doctors suggest patients get the flu shot. Flu viruses are always changing. So, the flu vaccine changes too. That means you need a new flu shot each year.

SCIENCE BREAKTHROUGH

In the 1940s, US doctors Thomas Francis Jr. and Jonas Salk created the first flu vaccine. The US Army was the first to receive it.

Jonas Salk

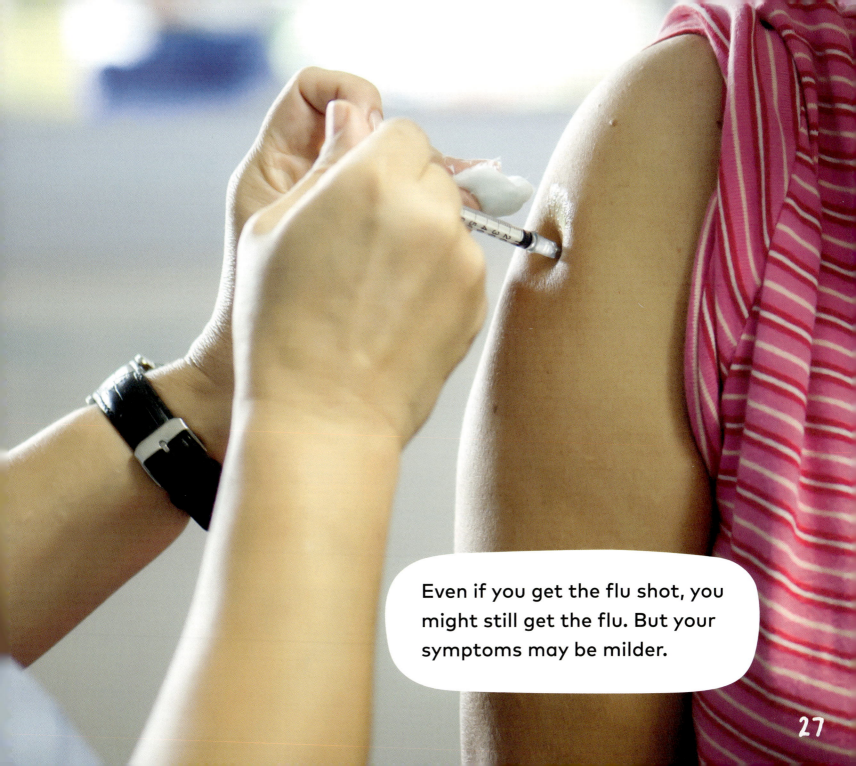

Even if you get the flu shot, you might still get the flu. But your symptoms may be milder.

HEALTHY HABITS

By practicing some healthy habits, you can help protect yourself from getting or spreading the flu.

- ☐ Keep a safe distance from sick people.
- ☐ Don't share dishes with people who are sick.
- ☐ Wash your hands often for at least 20 seconds with soap and water.
- ☐ Avoid touching your face.
- ☐ Cough and sneeze into tissues or your elbow.
- ☐ If you do get sick, stay home and rest! Wear a face mask if you must go out in public.

Influenza can be a harmful illness. But thanks to your amazing immune system, science, and some healthy habits, your body is ready to face these germ **invaders**!

GLOSSARY

chronic—when something occurs frequently or for a very long time.

complication—a second condition that develops during the course of a primary disease or condition.

contagious—a sickness that is spread by direct or indirect contact with an infected person or animal. A being with this sickness is also called contagious.

evidence—facts that prove something is true.

expose—to lay open for attack.

genetic—of or relating to a branch of biology that deals with inherited features.

hemisphere (HEH-muh-sfihr)—one half of the earth.

infect—to enter and cause disease in. Something or someone with a disease is infected, and the condition is called an infection.

inflame—to cause redness, heat, and pain.

invade—to enter and spread with the intent to take over. Something that does this is an invader.

mucus (MYOO-kuhs)—thick, slippery, protective fluid from the body.

organism—a living thing.

over-the-counter—available to purchase at stores without a doctor's prescription.

pandemic—occurring over a wide geographic area and affecting much of the population.

particle—a very small piece of matter, such as an atom or molecule.

release—to set free or let go.

RNA—ribonucleic acid, which is present in all living cells and carries the genetic information of many viruses.

sinus—a narrow, hollow tract in the skull that connects with the nostrils.

symptom—a noticeable change in the normal working of the body. A symptom indicates or accompanies disease, sickness, or other malfunction.

text—a written work.

ONLINE RESOURCES

To learn more about influenza, please visit **abdobooklinks.com** or scan this QR code. These links are routinely monitored and updated to provide the most current information available.

INDEX

Africa, 10
animals, 5

bacteria, 5,
breathing, 6, 12, 21, 24, 25
bronchitis, 24

chills, 16, 18
colds, 18, 19
complications, 22, 24, 25
coughing, 6, 7, 12, 16, 18, 21, 24, 25, 28
COVID-19, 11

doctors, 18, 22, 23, 25, 26

ears, 24
Europe, 10
eyes, 12, 25

face mask, 20, 28
fever, 7, 16, 18
flu season, 14, 15
Francis, Thomas, Jr., 26

headache, 16, 21
HIV/AIDS, 11

immune system, 7, 20, 26, 28
inflammation, 24

lungs, 8, 24, 25

mucus, 21, 24, 25
muscle aches, 16, 21

nose, 6, 8, 12, 18, 21, 25, 28

over-the-counter medicines, 21

pain, 16, 21, 24, 25
pandemic, 10, 11
plants, 5
pneumonia, 25
protozoa, 5

remedies, 21
replication, 7
respiratory system, 8
RNA, 6

Salk, Jonas, 26
SARS, 11
sinus infection, 25
sinuses, 6, 25
sneezing, 6, 7, 12, 18, 28
Spanish Flu, 11
spreading, 6, 7, 10, 11, 12, 13, 16, 20
stomach flu, 8
symptoms, 6, 7, 10, 12, 16, 18, 21, 24, 25, 27

throat, 8, 16, 18, 21
tiredness, 16, 18

United States, 8, 15, 26
US Army, 26

vaccines, 26, 27
viruses, 5, 6, 7, 8, 10, 11, 12, 14, 26

white blood cells, 7